In a Cast

Teaching Tips

Blue Level 4
This book focuses on the phonemes **/ow/ure/**.

Before Reading
- Discuss the title. Ask readers what they think the book will be about. Have them briefly explain why.
- Ask readers to sort the words on page 3. Read the sounds and words together.

Read the Book
- Encourage readers to break down unfamiliar words into units of sound. Then, ask them to string the sounds together to create the words.
- Urge readers to point out when the focused phonics phonemes appear in the text.

After Reading
- Encourage children to reread the book independently or with a friend.
- Ask readers to name other words with /ow/ or /ure/ phonemes. On a separate sheet of paper, have them write the words out.

© 2024 Booklife Publishing
This edition is published by arrangement with Booklife Publishing.

North American adaptations © 2024 Jump!
5357 Penn Avenue South
Minneapolis, MN 55419
www.jumplibrary.com

Decodables by Jump! are published by Jump! Library.
All rights reserved. No part of this book may be reproduced in any form without written permission from the publisher.

Library of Congress Cataloging-in-Publication Data is available at www.loc.gov or upon request from the publisher.

ISBN: 979-8-88996-825-2 (hardcover)
ISBN: 979-8-88996-826-9 (paperback)
ISBN: 979-8-88996-827-6 (ebook)

Photo Credits

Images are courtesy of Shutterstock.com. With thanks to Getty Images, Thinkstock Photo and iStockphoto. Cover - Lyakhova Evgeniya. 4–5 - Kekyalyaynen, Monkey Business Images. 6–7 – Science Photo Library, Sergey Ryzhov. 8–9 – Grzegorz Placzek, Rawpixel.com. 10–11 – Lyakhova Evgeniya, Yuganov Konstantin. 12–13 – ORION PRODUCTION. 14–15 – CandyBox Images, Kichigin. 16 – Shutterstock.

Can you sort all the words on this page into two groups?

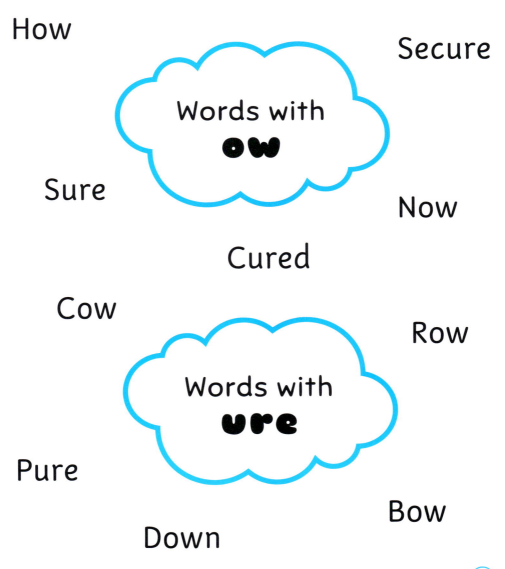

Her leg is in pain. How did she injure it? She fell off.

Can they cure her? They need to look at the leg to see if they can help.

If they are not sure what the problem is, they can get a picture.

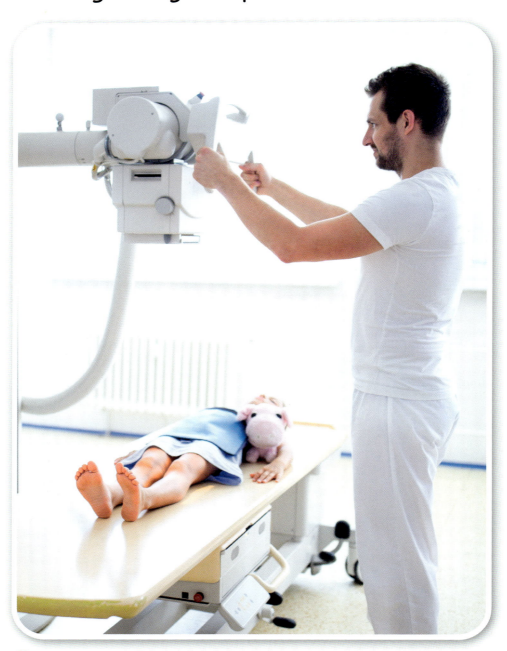

Will she need a gown? No, she can dress how she likes.

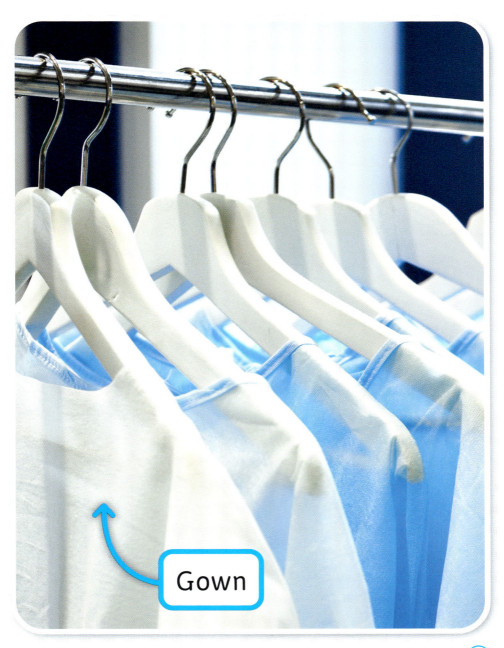

Gown

Now they are sure. There is a problem with her leg. It is a fracture.

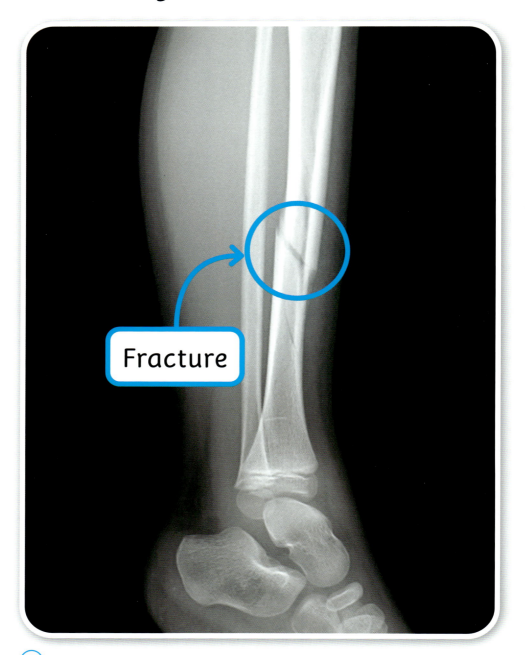

Fracture

She will need to get a cast on her leg.

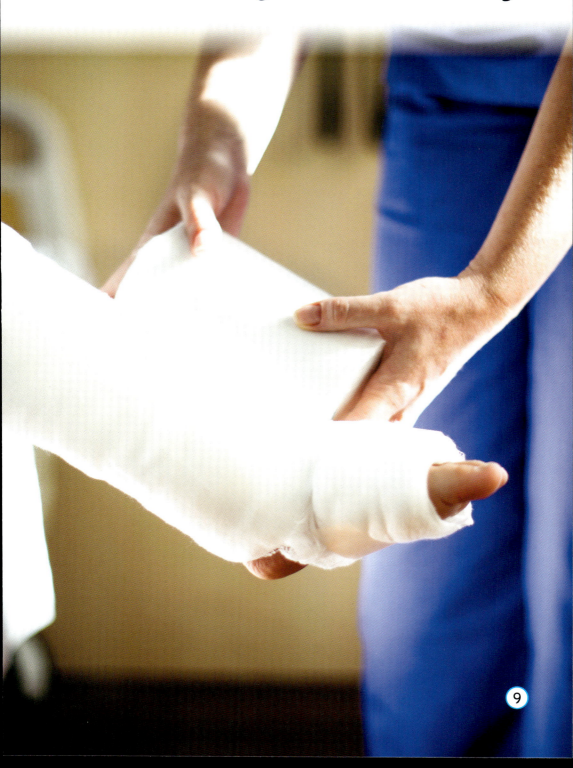

Now they can be sure that her leg will be kept still.

They will tell her how long the cast will need to be on her leg.

She must wait and allow the leg to rest. She must not run on it.

A cast can have pictures on it. You can color it with markers.

Her cast will be cut off when the leg is better.

She can run with no pain now.
They did cure her leg!

Sound out each word. Does it have an /ow/ or /ure/ sound?

flower

measure

owl

treasure